TEARS AND LAUGHTER
OF A MAN'S SOUL

BOOKS BY JAMES KAVANAUGH

NON-FICTION

There's Two Of You
Man In Search of God
Journal of Renewal
A Modern Priest Looks At His Outdated Church
The Struggle of the Unbeliever (Limited Edition)
The Birth of God
Between Man And Woman(co-authored)
Search: A Guide For Those Who Dare Ask Of Life
   Everything Good And Beautiful

POETRY

There Are Men Too Gentle To Live Among Wolves
Will You Be My Friend?
America: A Ballad
The Crooked Angel (a children's book)
Sunshine Days And Foggy Nights
Maybe If I Loved You More
Winter Has Lasted Too Long
Walk Easy On The Earth
Laughing Down Lonely Canyons
Today I Wondered About Love
   (Adapted from: Faces In The City)
From Loneliness To Love
Tears and Laughter Of A Man's Soul
Mystic Fire: The Love Poetry Of
   James Kavanaugh
Quiet Water: The Inspirational Poetry of
   James Kavanaugh

FICTION

A Coward For Them All
The Celibates

ALLEGORY

Celebrate The Sun: A Love Story
A Village Called Harmony - A Fable

TEARS AND LAUGHTER
OF A MAN'S SOUL

JAMES KAVANAUGH

ILLUSTRATIONS BY REGINA ANTONIA-TRISTAN

STEVEN J. NASH PUBLISHER
P.O. BOX 2115
HIGHLAND PARK, ILLINOIS

Designed by Cheryl Pecaut
Cover Design: Dick James

Library of Congress Cataloging in Publication Data

Kavanaugh, James
  Tears And Laughter Of A Man's Soul
    1. Title

Library of Congress Catalogue #90-062061
ISBN #1-878995-08-1

---

10 9 8 7 6 5 4 3 2

ACKNOWLEDGMENTS:

My gratitude to Cheryl Pecaut and Vicki Gioscio,

To Don Biggs and Dick James.

DEDICATION:

To those who seem to have lost their way
And are forever determined to find it.

To those who know that darkness and death
Are but imposters leading to light and life.

INTRODUCTION

Men are not easy to know even by other men. We learn to hide
feelings at an early age until denial and pretense become a way of
life. Thus our rite of passage is not a gentle one, especially since
there is little guidance in the shaping of our hearts and minds.

It is a rare woman who understands men, since we learn to hide
what seems too risky to reveal, and thus deny our very manhood
to have peace. We learn early on our morality is controlled by
women, and even our schools favor traditionally feminine
virtues. This is not to blame women nor to defend our
masquerade. It is only to admit a male mystique that locks us
painfully within ourselves.

Assuredly, men do not have a unique claim on pain, but our male
bravado offers us fewer outlets to vent it. We hide it from wives
and colleagues, and usually from ourselves. Even therapists must
patiently drag it out of us. Only a vague, persistent malaise
suggests the toll that is taken by jobs and lifestyles we never
really wanted. We are taught to compete as a way of life, burying
feelings in compulsive work, and surrendering joy and freedom to
the safety of a monotonous life. And in response to feminist
attacks, we become more docile and even less ourselves.

Hardly aware of our own inner anguish, we gradually lose our
masculine courage to become docile drones of the dreams and
appetites of others. We surrender the male strength that is the
very source of our creativity and independence. We become
slaves of an often inhuman economy and give up the innate gifts
which make us men. When we slowly and helplessly lose control
of our lives, we try to salvage them by angrily controlling others.
Only an awareness of our real feelings can begin to free us. More
often than not, we do not know what we feel, and thus are
severed from our true identity as men.

Often we hope that another marriage, a secret affair, or greater income will revive us, only to discover that ingrained habits but assume a new addictive form. More work replaces less alcohol, depression fills the vacuum of dead dreams, and a carefully concealed fear grows more tangible and destructive. We feel all alone. The jogging or golf that once brought us back to life have grown stale. When we do not know where to turn, physical health often becomes a new obsession. We are victims of the only choices we were able to make, and starting over seems impossible.

In truth the path to freedom and joy, though initially painful, is more exciting than difficult. At the root, I believe the problem is a spiritual one, but we begin by uncovering feelings that were buried since boyhood. When we don't know our own true emotions, it is little wonder that our job or marriage was never a genuine choice. We learned to be ashamed of who we really are, and guilty about the very passion that makes us unique and masculine. Even God is a lie until a wall of private illusions is torn down by an honest acceptance of our real feelings.

Like many men, I am still on my journey, but now I know that the blood and bruises of retracing steps and beginning again will not destroy me. They give me new strength and brighter hope in a life that was losing meaning. They illumine the dark depression that tried anything to learn that nothing on earth was enough. Finally, the man that is emerging seems like me, with a growing faith in the quiet, Inner Voice that is far more than dogmatic ideas and ancient arguments.

This is a book of reflections I wrote during these last few years of my journey. Although I wrote them to myself, I share them with you in the hope that my laughter and tears along the way might somehow bring you courage. The caring words of friends have helped me when I feared I might give up. Perhaps my words can do the same for you. I promise you this is not a book of rhetoric, but a saga of life and near death, victory and defeat, falling and rising. It is above all the *Tears And Laughter Of A Man's Soul*.

James Kavanaugh
Chicago

CHILDHOOD DREAMS

"...the dreams you refuse to abandon
   will explode with new life,
Taller than the mountains, brighter
   than the sun..."

OF CHILDHOOD DREAMS

No one need abandon childhood dreams that outlive
    dry illusions
      Born of fear and other's hoarded expectations.
There is but one lesson to learn, as easy as squirrels
    and sunshine,
A lesson echoed endlessly in whispers in the sanctuary
    of your heart,
      No matter how long or far you have strayed.
To ignore it is the only sin, a tragic guarantee that
    Sadness and emptiness will haunt the final days
    of your life.
Though the mountains fall on you and the sky denies
    her light,
Though the moon disappear and clouds are troubled
    and angry,
All of this will pass away no matter the time or season.

Then the dreams you refused to abandon will explode
    with new life.
    Taller than the mountains, brighter than the sun,
And the joyful song that was yours from the beginning
    Will resound across the silver edges of your
    days and nights,
And lead you lovingly and fearlessly into the light.

A CHILD STILL WANDERING

A child still wandering the woods of my own mind,
Still afraid of the dark, but not wanting to walk
  In what most others call the light,
His eyes devour life
  Excited at each latest motion of the leaves,
  Thanking the breeze that cools his cheeks on a
    hot summer day,
  Creating like a deity every new wonder that he sees.
Teach me, my child!
  And I will never again let go of your hand.
Take me back where the flash of a trout at creek's edge
    Could take my breath away.
Lead me to the wonder of baby rabbits hiding timidly
    In the deep spring grass,
When each step along a familiar path was a new vision,
  Each sunset a burst of ecstasy,
  Each unfamiliar sound a song of unexpected joy.
All I ask of those I tried to love, I now ask of you.
  You were the gentle guide I lost to manhood,
  The friend I've longed for and never really found.
    The eyes and ears that time and trafficing took away,
  Which men and women painfully pursue this very day,
  And only a wandering child can reveal the way.

(One morning I woke from a dream in which I saw myself as a kind of collective man who had unwittingly gathered the harshest and most abusive remnants of parents and teachers into a stern, abusive critic of my own child. I knew that this cruel, carping adult hiding in my consciousness had to be challenged head-on by the forgiving and compassionate man I was trying to become. I made a cup of coffee and wrote this poem while the shadows of my dream still lingered.)

FRIGHTENING MAN

Frightening man of the past, darkest shadow on earth,
  Gouging the light from an eager child's eyes, and
  Blinding his joyful vision with scarred ugliness,
Who made you guardian of tender hope and fragile dreams,
Who let your rasping words terrify virginal sensitivities,
  And private rage smother bubbling energies, when
    I was but a step from innocence and wild flowers?
I was without greed or guile or guilt, I could have
  Transformed cities and led children to the light
    Like a Pied Piper of the sunrise?
Birds talked to me, the wet grass whispered its secrets,
  Trees stooped to stroke me in the wind as I passed.

Even now you claw at my consciousness, arrogantly hoping
To recreate past terror at the sound of your footsteps,
  Snarling and hissing of death when there is but life.
Too late! The man will brush away your very breath, free
  From nightmares helplessly inherited in childhood,
Leaving you in comic nakedness of a bogey-man costume
  That finally seems silly in the sunshine.
As man and boy at last run laughing through the land,
  To sing their song of freedom, hand in hand!

WOUNDED CHILD

Wounded child, killing me with scars of your
   ancient imprisonment!
Your buried, rescuing rage has finally been heard by me,
   Your silent tears, as acceptable as winter storms,
     have finally been shed and wiped away!
No longer must you tremble before giant males
     with thunderous voices and deaf ears. I am here!
No longer the whining females and craven cassocks that lived
   their cowardice through your incredible courage.
   I am here!
You are my only child, not another little boy to love,
   No competition, always enough time to hear your pain
   and to soften every fear.
   Now there's time to play and laugh, little boy, and
   leave the whores and wars to me.
At long last I am strong enough for you to be safe,
   Erect enough to hold you in solid arms and
   square shoulders.
You are my boy, my beloved boy, no more a fractured
   spoiled child, impulsively asking recompense
     for all the pain.
I am in charge, the worries are finally all mine!
   How I love to watch you laugh, catch tadpoles and
   hide like an Indian in the deep grass,
   Scare me with garter snakes and blinking frogs.
Trust me, child, play till I put you to bed, sing you
   lullabies, and kiss you good night.
I am in charge now, little boy, and I love you, finally
   I love you, as no one else ever could!

LET A CHILD EMERGE

Time to let go of fear and let a child emerge,
Time to admit anxieties which are deep rooted
    In a boy's timidity,
Struggling to be the man he feigned to be.
Shyness is no vice, nor trembling,
Fear is no sin, nor the struggle to be brave when
    There is little reason.
Surrender to what is, face it patiently and clearly,
And make friends with a self you've trampled on
    Running towards some impossible success.
The moon still stares lovingly even behind clouds,
The stars still call you to serenity,
Children still laugh and dogs lap your hand.
Abandon the struggle, let everyone win who needs to!
Be content to live with feebleness and patience and fear
    That comes and goes like the wind.
Do not be love's slave, but find a heart
    As clear and gentle as your own,
Where words are never uttered to alter your being,
    Or challenge your very existence.
The let go of fear and let a child emerge!

(On a recent plane trip, I sat next to a little boy drawing those pictures made with connecting dots and numbers. After each success, the young Michaelangelo had to share his wonders with me. Soon I forgot about my pre-boarding fantasy of sitting next to a soft-spoken, loving woman who would hand me her heart over Albuquerque. The kid was wonderful! After he got off and generously handed me several of his "favorite" pictures, I wrote this poem.)

BY THE NUMBERS

I'm drawing me now — finally —
Like a child going from number to number,
   Hoping, trusting somehow that a picture
      will appear,
A picture of me
   I've not seen since very early childhood.

MAN-CHILD

Beyond plans of success and dreams of affluence,
  Beyond threats and boasts and seeming confidence,
I see your fear and know that when you lose your boyhood,
  You lose what makes you warm and attractive as a man.
Life is not lived in spurts
  Where manhood destroys boyhood like some
    major surgery never to be undone.
I love not your obvious triumphs and heady expertise,
  But a laughing, playful, awkward boy, unchained and
    unpredictable, who can drop everything to hear
  A distant seal trumpeting on the midnight rocks,
Or watch the messy swallow building his mortared nest,
  Fouling picture windows and garage doors
    like a demented mason.
When the boy is gone, the man is all drive and head,
  Without arms and legs, without eyes and ears and
    some explosive joy.

There is no life as fine as spontaneity and passion.
  No success to match a vibrant energy of life,
And assuredly, none more beautiful than one who moves
  Bravely beyond the hungry needs of boyhood,
To stay in daily, loving contact with his inner child.

WANTING SOMEONE

"Wanting someone to know the whole story
  Without retelling it
    in clumsy, leaking words,
And to love me completely in spite of it all."

(I wrote this one winter evening after walking for hours in the snow, searching for an answer to a stubborn wave of loneliness. I admitted to myself that I was living with the illusions of my youth and a deceitful culture. I was seeking someone to put me together, though I knew this had never worked in the past. I went inside, lit a fire, and wrote words from my soul.)

WANTING SOMEONE

Wanting someone to know the whole story
    Without retelling it in clumsy, leaking words,
Then to love me completely in spite of it all.
How many Spring loves have abandoned me
    To survive the Winter!
How many illusions have passed away when time
    Seemed forever!
Illusions are the luxury of youth when
    A high income or low golf score seemed enough
    And assorted lovers were as easy to enjoy as apples.
Would that love and joy might come leaping over the hill
    At my crisp command!
Would that courage and confidence might remain at levels
    I have intermittently known
        With less reason than I have today!
If this dullness is to disappear
    And the grey pallor sickening all that is beautiful
        Is to dissolve,
I must begin again and again to live in honesty,
    Taking joy only from what is really mine,
Till even my most persistent illusions get the word.

THE LADY

Well, the lady wasn't really beautiful,
   But she was to me.
Some warmth and gentleness from deep inside
   That promised not to hurt me.
I've hurt enough
   And refuse to know it one more time.
For awhile I thought
   I'd spend my days
      with butterflies and hummingbirds,
   Catching a few fireflies again,
And walk the streets
   Writing my poems
      like I've done a hundred times before.
I think I could make it with her,
   So much love to give
      to someone as gentle and frightened as I am.
Tomorrow I'll ask her, straight out,
   And if she turns away,
      I know she'll do it gently with a smile.
And there's always the hummingbirds.

REGINA AND ME

Well, Regina's proud of her new executive office and
  The perks that once were the sole property of men,
And I'm just as proud of my new recipe for
  Tuna casserole, and the way Spray 'n Wash takes
  pizza stains out of my sport shirts.
Regina reads the Wall St. Journal, Money Magazine,
  Forbes, and The U.S. News And World Report.
I read the Green Grocer, Better Homes and Gardens,
  And pay much closer attention to the detergent
  commercials on TV.
This is all in the name of a wonderful new world!

Now, she can make it without me picking up tabs
  And paying the bills,
And I can get along without her cooking my food and
  Doing my shirts. (God, I love that Spray 'n Wash)
The only problem is that we can't figure out what
  we have in common,
  Which is what started this whole revolution
  in the first place.
I can't stand Money Magazine or the boring
  Wall Street Journal,
  And she never answers when I brag about my
  all color bleach.
So we decided just to drift apart in the name of
  personal liberation.
The only part that really rankles is that she's been
  telling everyone
I used her just to get her recipe for tuna casserole.

My one relationship with an angry feminist had a happy ending,
but in her transition, I was newly the enemy. I had no quarrel
with her right to hostility, as long as it wasn't aimed at me. Her
rage at men roused my buried anger towards women. Our
conflict inspired this poem when I could honestly express my
feelings.

JANELLE

I look sadly, Janelle, at the buttress of a mortared jaw,
The dark moat of a lipless mouth made mad and murky
    by history's sewage,
Your tongue a rusted drawbridge screaming for revenge,
Your nose a cautious watchtower forbidding laughter,
Your cheeks high, unscaleable walls barely
    distinguishing friend from invader,
Your eyes flashing with unhealed and unrelenting anger
    of a grieving sisterhood.
Your very body a knight's armor, guarding iron breasts
    finally safe and untouchable,
Your mind drenching intruders with boiling memories
    sucked from every crevice of the past,
Your heart a deadbolt of suspicion and hate, your sex
    hoarded like miserly gold to support costly illusions,
And I am sad for you, Janelle!

You are pain's cadaverous trophy with honed syllables
    and mordant wit,
With the fierce, judgmental scars of a frozen femininity
    that bludgeons real men,
And finds, instead, a male mannequin to reshape like
    a pale, stammering MacBeth
Apologizing for timid testicles, and meekly assigning
    your caustic madrigals to himself,
Selling his effeminate manhood for a child's bowl
    of nippled porridge.

15

I have outgrown the naughty girl protests and assaults
   Of an emasculating sisterhood.
Your pubic gate is forever safe from my battering ram,
   your castle in no danger of violation.
Once I waited outside like a timid page, pleading for
   Maid Marian's rescuing favors.
Now, I stand as a man, wanting to love a woman, but not
   willing to woo her at the cost of my soul.

I do not question your pain, Janelle, for I have too
   long endured my own,
Blaming, like a helpless boy, every mother and daughter
   who scorned my festering flaccidity,
Manipulating any nanny who refused to nurse adolescent
   and addicting anguish,
Fighting to control what I dared not do without,
   surrendering integrity to petulant puberty,
Flaunting my vaunted power to the very degree that I
   felt frightened of your strength.
No longer!
I am as much time and culture's victim as you, Janelle,
   assuredly as innocent and angry,
As much an indentured slave of commerce, as you of
   children and domestic drudgery,
As resentful of man's premature demise, as you of
   woman's degrading bondage,
As strong and determined, as bruised and unheard, as
   used and misunderstood as you are.

It is time not to rage but to talk, not to judge but
   to hear, not to accuse but to see!
To move beyond petulance and pouting to the mutual
   respect and genuine freedom
Of a mature man and woman profoundly in love!

SOME LUSTRE

There is some lustre gone from your eyes
  That yesterday was there,
Some dream darkened until it disappeared,
Some hope eclipsed, some fantasy drained of blood
  by dull reality.
I have come to restore your joy, to give you back
  the mountains and oceans, and squirrels
    chattering in forests.
To teach you once again to count the stars,
  Rejoice at the sight of flowers,
  Exclaim at the fragrance of the Eucalyptus.
Look around at the intense and pale faces,
  The grim lips and tired eyes,
And know that life without love and dreams
  Is only a duty to be performed, a trail to follow,
  A dull, enduring highway that leads nowhere.
I have travelled it long enough!
Now I want to bring back the lustre to your eyes,
  So that together we do not miss a single rainbow
  Or lose our sense of wonder at the silence
      of mountains
    and the silver ocean shimmering in moonlight.
And most of all that we do not surrender our love
  To neon and net worth and a dawn
That is only the beginning of another empty day.

WINGS

I let you take my wings briefly away
   And chirped appropriately like a jungle bird encaged,
Entertaining on command and singing sometimes sweetly
   For my supper like a frightened nightingale,
But serenading not half so well as when I soared
   Freely in the trees, and loved you
      In the solitude and silence of my fondest flying.
Why did you never understand?
   There is no cage large enough
   No captor powerful enough
   No chain strong enough to hold me.
I would die before I would finally surrender!
Even a bird cannot be possessed, and if freedom
      is his birthrite,
   So much the more it is mine,
And neither he nor I are swayed when even the mountains
   Are content to be captive.
We build our nest where we are,
   Lost only without the sun and sudden rain,
   Desolate only without the moon, or the hissing
      of a wind rattling October leaves.
We have known such joy all by ourselves
   That no melody could contain our rejoicing.
We can fly even without wings, sing even when strangled,
   And outlive any zookeeper,
Even those who were appointed to love us.

OF FRIENDSHIP
AND ADDICTION

Finally I let go, but not one second before I had to.
I had caused you pain enough a hundred times over,
  And caused myself pain as deep and unyielding.
You were mother, father, childhood, family
  To a smiling, frightened boy who feared the dark
    without you,
  And could not face his life alone.
It is not uncommon to let go of a unique friendship
  And thus to lose one's own way for a time.
But this very raking of the soul was new to me, and
  Just to hang on seemed the only way to survive.
I could not end it one second before because you were
  The one and only home I ever had.
Now orphaned, and too old and proud to be adopted,
  I must find that home in my heart,
And step by step somehow I will, but losing you is like
  Losing my way in the darkest forest of childhood,
Alone in a tornado, abandoned in churning ocean waters.
Now is our freedom, an end to the unbearable pain
  That left us both in blood and tatters.

Call it what you will, call me what you will!
  It does not matter. No one is really to blame,
    save scars at conception and birth.
What seems courage may be fear and anger from the past,
What seems dishonesty may be but hurt and terror
    from childhood.
It is only important that it is over,
  Whether it ever be understood or forgiven, for now
Two bruised children finally have a chance to live!

LOVE AT DAWN

I have crawled down strange, cobblestone streets,
   And persistently climbed uncompromising mountains,
Outlasted storm clouds and survived murky swamplands,
   Galloped through dry fields laden with rocks,
And swam bottomless lakes of icy water all alone.
   Only love has consistently eluded me, and at dawn today
I feared that it may never again be mine,
   That I waited too long, moved too slowly,
Spent too much time in wild adventuring
   And not enough time in patient romance.
Yet, I do not regret my life with its excitement,
   And even the very pain that guides my healing.
I only know that for now I will sacrifice
   A few pointless detours and distant curiosities
For the close embrace of a true and lasting love,
   And a gentle, loving companion, fashioned for me
By the laughing quirk of a loving God, and appointed
   For the remaining miles of a very joyful journey.

SOUL-MATE

You are all eyes of wonder and joy,
   Daughter of spring and beloved clown of summer,
Destined to make children laugh and me smile,
   Created to make my life full and wondrous.
I hold you at night, cradled like satin and sunshine
   in my arms,
My eyes never tire of exploring you, teasing you,
   leading you to the moonlit crest of mountains.
How did I live without you?
   How many charades accepted in lieu of you?
You are a child of dawn, a first crocus promising the
   demise of winter.
Once sex was so important, orgasm so beaded with sweat
   and significance.
Now a glance can fill my soul and move me profoundly
   to thank the god of all good gifts.
How long I have waited, scanned distant horizons and
   combed the backroads for you,
And imagined you in every color the sun's circuit
   made available.
Only when I finally gained entrance into the sealed
   corridors of my own soul,
Did I discover you in my backyard, sitting under a
   childhood cherry tree,
Softly smiling with eyes I never before saw, until
   I could look quietly and lovingly into my own.

I HAVE LOVED

I have loved my share of women
   Across the country and the world,
Pursued some and defended myself against others.
Only hoping that one who had walked where I have walked,
   Might understand the twilight and the trees,
Might remember poignantly the thorns and rocks
   And precipices too steep to climb.
Love is difficult but not impossible for those
   Who refuse to surrender to routine isolation,
And feel loneliness in the midst of our culture's
   Most exalted models of what life is supposed to be.
They have the house and spouse, the kids and dog,
   The boat and Caribbean vacations.
They have financial security and someone to call
     day or night
   To chase the spectres away.
I try to settle for that, and sometimes wish I had,
   Accepting security for a unique attention,
Bargaining away my soul in hope that some magical woman
   Will put the pieces together to create my life.
Now I know that the pieces are in my own hand,
   And the puzzle is only difficult, not impossible.

OF DESTINY AND DETOURS

*"What kind of world ignores sunsets and the laughter
of God,
Never lies on the grass or softens at twilight?
. . . I no longer measure a world by what it possesses,
but by what brings peace,
And by all the things in life it really doesn't need."*

WHAT KIND OF WORLD

What kind of world
  Ignores sunsets and the laughter of God,
  Never lies on the grass or softens at twilight?

What kind of world
  Is afraid to be alone and devours any love
  Like a drowning sailor grasping for driftwood?

Don't you know
  The skies and hills are a drama composed for you,
  That sunrise and seas are a theatre for those
    who would never afford Broadway?

I no longer measure a world
  But what it possesses,
    But by what brings peace,
  And by all the things in life
    It really doesn't need.

USED FURNITURE ADS AND DREAMS

Dreams for sale every day!
  The fake Tiffany that fooled Margaret's mother,
    And the pecan bedroom set with a leopard spread
    that couldn't wait to undress.
There's the redwood coffee table Mike carved from a
  giant burl in the days Donna knew he
    really loved her,
The proud stroller Pete once guided through shaded
  streets and smiling neighbors, and
    Dawn forgot about her drunken parents.
A pair of skis from Christmas in the Colorado pines,
Records from the fifties when Jack and Dora
  drank and danced till closing time,
Then left to make crazy, lusting, half-drunk love on the
  lambskin rug they're letting go for six bucks.
There's a sofa or two that conceived at least one baby,
  and another that caressed a dying parent,
An easy chair rises like King Arthur's throne, a relic
  of days when Ed was king, when cold beer and
    Jean's lasagna were keys to a private heaven.
There's the pool table they couldn't afford, ten speeds
  from when they still cared about staying in shape,
A hanging lamp Patti made of gelatin and egg cartons,
  and Jim bragged about even to his buddies,
The Budweiser sign, the antique meat grinder, even
  an old suitcase with London and Paris
    glued on forever.

Dreams are for sale every day and a buck or two will
    get you the laughs and tears of a lifetime because
Yesterday's dreams are cheap. It's today's that
  cost so much.

COMPUTER WORLD

Computer world!
  Surrendering truth and beauty to the demands of time
  And the cold, simplistic language of machines,
  Curtailing the refinements of adverbs and adjectives.
    Imagination frozen on a desolate keyboard.
  Software junkies putter like mechanics of yesteryears,
  Left-brain monks living in safe, codified boundaries,
    Finally taking revenge on a lonely childhood.
  War is now a word locked safely on voiceless discs
    Accessible only to the elect,
Buried or retrieved by the defacing of an angry key!
No dead boys or broken lives, no childrens' screams,
  No widows or anguished mothers carrying
  An indelible, bloody memory to their unmarked graves!

Computer world!
  Surrendering truth and beauty to the demands of time
    And the cold, simplistic language of machines,
  Where life is an extension of bottom lines and robots
    Leaping from screens to walk among us.

Literature has no place or music, only barren sounds
   Propagating the frozen facts that rule the earth,
As if wisdom can be contained in cold, cryptic menus
   And tasteless symbols mocking singularity.
Anthropoids who, in dramatic evolution, fought their
   Way from water to land, now return to
Galley ship and cotton field, sacrificing creativity
   To conformity, surrendering brave pioneering
To the empty adoration of an unforgiving machine,
   Shorn of sovereignty and expansive dreams.

Computer world!
   The soft chorus of keys, a slave's shoulders bowed,
      And empty eyes fixed on a master's screen
   Without sympathy or sunshine, freedom or independence
      In the controlling, colorless galaxy of
Computer world!

ANDROIDS

Man from another time,
Wondering what fiends divert computers
    To take away privacy
    To celebrate isolation
    To abandon feeling
Android clerks run hotels or airlines or drug stores,
And people line up like machines to fly or buy,
    Or eat, perhaps to die
In decent order without troubling the machines
    Or their unknowing operators.

Man from another time,
Get the hell out of here while there are still
    hills and meadows and an unpolluted stream.
Gaze at the last eagle outside a zoo,
Watch the diving osprey freer than most men,
And see the baby snakes slither in the May sun
    as gentle as rabbits.
Abandon freeways and airways, overpriced restaurants
    and obscene hotels,
And cities where the land is as costly as gold.

Man from another time, part cowboy, part drifter,
    part poet and hobo, lover, renegade, and man-child,
Why do you live in slavery when the whole world
    is your playground?

HOW CAN THEY BE
SO HAPPY

How can they be so happy,
 Mexican fruit pickers with three kids under five,
 Immigrants mopping garages bigger than their whole house,
 Vagrants who walk two miles to find a restroom,
 Janitors who can't spell Oleg Cassini or Calvin Klein?
How can they be so happy,
 Jobless blacks screaming at a football game on TV,
 Weary laborers who can't send a kid to college,
 Grinning doormen who can't afford a dentist,
 Men washing cars who never had one of their own?
How can they be so happy,
 When Elvis seemed as miserable as Howard Hughes,
 And even ole man Rockefeller didn't seem
  the picture of joy?

Sometimes Bel Air and Lake Forest, Montauk and Malibu,
Greystones and brownstones, and the sprawling palaces
 Of mediocre actors and fleeting rock stars,
Seem lonelier and more dismal than Harlem and Waats,
 And maybe there's a reason I confuse Forest Hills
  with Forest Lawn.
Lately I'm changing my attitude about happiness, and
 taking a closer look at simplicity.
Christmas madness finally escaped me, exorbitant
 restaurants seem as vulgar as decorator homes.
Ski lodges don't seem half as much fun as snow shoes
 and lavish hotels remind me of lonely mausoleums.

Soon enough the sons of boat people will own my house,
   and blacks will fight Koreans for Beverly Hills.
Meanwhile, it's revealing, that amid movers and shakers,
   Tycoons and skyscrapers and electric entrepreneurs,
The happiest man I saw today was shining my shoes
   in a basement barber shop.

OF LIFE AND MONEY MAGAZINE

According to *Money Magazine*, Wilbur Ames lives in the
    next to the worst sizeable city in America,
Even though he loves pruning bushes for the county,
    Plowing fresh snow on crisp, moonlit nights,
      and dragging leaves from the drains and gutters.
Most of all he loves the spring when roses
    come back to life,
Baby birds gawk from nests, gophers play tag, and
    Squirrels thank God the acorns held out
      for another winter.
Wilbur never frets over the greenhouse factor,
    ozone layers,
    Or the devaluation of the dollar in Tokyo.
He's concerned when his tomatoes are slow to ripen,
    The National Geographic arrives a week late,
    And the homeless sleep in the parks - even though
    Two regulars now enjoy the splendor of his garage.
He's learning Spanish from his Mexican assistant,
    Is a dedicated rock hound, haunts garage sales, and
    Has read everything Twain and Steinbeck ever wrote.
Wilbur hasn't locked his doors in twenty years,
    Raised his kids in gentleness and fertilizing love,
    And never fussed with Dorothy about the rights
      of women or the stressful life of men.

He preaches no philosophy, ignores psychology, and
   Attends the same church his parents did, because
   He loves to sing and the cinnammon rolls
      at Marvin's Cafe
   Taste better after the ten o'clock service.
He seldom hears the news, gave up TV sports years ago,
   Classifies Wall Street and politics with soap operas
   and Saturday morning cartoons.
But he knows the wind's smile, the scowl of
      threatening clouds,
   The smell of the sugarpine forest, the contented
      gurgle of a stream swollen by winter runoffs,
   And the thick, lazy air that announces the sudden
      arrival of spring,
Grateful that his wife's bread still tastes of wheat,
   Her strong coffee still softens the bite of winter,
   And that Boots, his old black lab, still shuffles
      to greet him every night after work.
Grateful above all that Dorothy still looks at him
      with love, and the kids never miss a
      Thanksgiving dinner
In the next to the worst sizeable city
   in the whole country.

OF CRITICS

The critics gather like vultures masquerading as eagles,
   Feasting on carrion from their own flesh,
      Knowing it has grown sour and tasteless
         as their decaying dreams.
   Raging their vengeance against those with the courage
         to share a simple meal of abiding hope.
   How many bodies have they disemboweled?
   How many young creators turned to silent stone
      With viscious words that tell far more
         of private pain than what they criticized?
      Afraid to live their own dreams, forever unaware
         of what life asks.
They are the assassins of independent thought, the real
   Murderers of energy and hope, the bloody ghosts
      Of parents and teachers who etched their
         angry memories of fear upon creative courage,
      Ready to extoll acclaimed and acceptable strangers,
   But timidly mocking their own children
         into silent conformity,
      Even as they scream from the depths of a blighted hope:
         "You are no more than me! You cannot be!"
         "You cannot be! You must not be!"
"Don't you understand?"

SPEAKING BANK

I don't speak "bank", though German is easy if you
   watch a few World War II movies, and enough
Tequilla, can make *enchiladas* and *cerveza*, spoken
   quickly, sound like quite irresistible foreplay.
" Bank", like French, has too damn many irregular verbs.
   A simple loan transaction is never what it appears,

Like when my blunt buddy, Frog Davis, applied for one:
   "Hi, pal. I heard your TV ad! I wanna rent some money!"
   "I presume you want a loan?"
   "What's the rent?"
   "You are asking about our current interest rate?"
   "You want first and last, or just a deposit?"
   "I trust you mean points, sir? Do you have an account with us?"
   "I don't have shit! That's why I wanna rent some dough."
   "I'm afraid *we* can't, help you, sir."
   "Forget the rest of 'em. How about you and the
      fat guy on your TV ad?"
   "Can you offer collateral, sir?"
   "As soon as I rent the money, I can."
   "The point is, sir, we don't know you."
   "I know that. That's why the hell I came in!"
   "Sir, this is getting quite ridiculous."
   "Not to me. I thought you guys rented money."
   "We make appropriate loans with suitable collateral."
   "Where the hell's the fat guy? You take Mobil cards?"
   "I'm afraid not. We accept collateral from people we know."
   "Would it help if I were black? The fat guy said..."
   "Race or sex is not of consequence, sir."

"But tubby said you just needed a signature."
"If we can establish your credit rating."
"Call the bastards! I don't owe nobody nothing."
"I would like to help you, sir. You seem very sincere!"
"You don't rent to sincere people?"
"No, sir... or yes, sir... I mean..."
"Hey, you look like hell, man! Will the fat guy
    be in tomorrow?"

AT MARINO'S

Things don't change much at *Marino's Steak House*
  Along the two-lane highway dividing farm from farm,
And leading to the placid lakes where tourists flock
  To make the natives insane and transform good people
    into greedy summertime landlords.
Marino's, meanwhile, stays about the same with sloe gin
  And draft Mick, and a quarter-inch filet fixed
    medium-rare only on a computer.
But at least you can count on something stable
  in your life
When the market goes bust and the evening news
  assures you
There won't be enough oil and clean water if we survive,
  Or enough morphine or cyanide if we don't.

So when the sky is grey and the sun is filtered
    by the haze of man's madness,
When the ways of an avaricious world crowd your mind
    Until you wonder far into daylight what it all means,
Just stop worrying and have a Mick at Marino's,
    Dress up your giant baked potato in cholesterol,
Take your skinny filet from a loving, local waitress
    Who still blushes like a pink peony, sip
      your powerful coffee, maybe even smoke
        a forbidden cigarette, and know,
No matter what, life's still gonna be okay at Marino's.

My friend, Jim "Two-Bits" O'Dea always seemed different. He has a quiet style I admire, as if in touch with peace that eluded me. One day in a park, the silence got to me and I asked him about the trial of a lawyer who beat his girl friend's kid to death. "I didn't hear about it", though it was news for weeks. "Why hear about a poor kid I can't help?" He left me reflecting for a long time.

OUT OF THE NEWS

Two-bits O'Dea told me:
He finally learned to ignore headlines and hysterical
    news reports that have
    About as much to do with life as the United Nations.
Like if the Dow Jones drops a century or heads for 3000,
    Who cares when you haven't owned a stock since Edsel?
And why sweat preachers or politicians and their bimbos
    When you haven't trusted 'em since Christ and Lincoln?
And why hear about wars when your wife's beating cancer,
    And your old yellow hound made it for another winter?
Or screw trade deficits when ears can still hear Mozart
    And eyes still see mountains laughing in the moonlight!
And so what if liberated women blame men for breathing
    When your lady thinks you rule the sun's itinerary?
Or who really cares about the greedy larceny of a Marcos,
    When you know how Ford and Rockefeller built empires?
And why hear about a national debt or weak dollar, when
    Your kid loves his job and calls you 'cause he cares?
Or why read about gang wars, purse snatchers, and rapes
    When you still spend more time laughing than crying?

While it's nice to read that a cabbie won the lottery,
　Or a blind man, mugged on the subway, got his sight,
Soon the commentators shout about an empty arms accord
　And TV screams of a rock star who may survive summer.
Meantime it helps to ease the edges of a lonely night
　With quiet talk or lingering walks with good friends,
Guarded from pain I didn't cause and hurt I can't erase,
　Deeply grateful that there will be no damn headlines!

OF NEW AGE CLAIRVOYANCE

*In my struggle to find truth, I met an astute Irish guru who
insisted we all began as daffodils, later to emerge as squid, then
yaks or crocodiles depending on our overbite. After six earth
planes, the elect entered a phase of spiritual bulemia, where food
and sex were acutely toxic. The guru himself was well into the 7th
plane. No one asked our enlighted guide how he knew all this,
since the brochure said he had met Ayn Rand, lived with Ghandi
for a week, was once on the Tonight Show, and got five big ones
for a weekend seminar. I didn't suspect it might be a big business
until weeks later Big Louie Vaskowitz began wearing a toga.*

BIG LOUIE

Big Louie Vaskowitz, the roughest guy I know and liberator
   of 67 virgins in a 12 block area,
Told me he bought his own channeler, who puts him in touch with
   an East Indian cobra salesman who died broke after a brutal,
      all night crap game under a full moon in Bangladesh.
Louie thinks he's connected since he not only predicts
   the future, but picked a 30 to 1 gelding at Hawthorn,
And made Louie the fastest 20 grand since he sold
   a carload of condoms allegedly blessed by the pope.

And Slim Davis, the best jitterbugger I ever knew
   and an ace in the Korean conflict,
Has a healing crystal for every occasion from a complex
   headache to a simple homicide,
And while scientists slave to solve a variety
   of sexual plaints,
Slim found the answer with a purple crystal

that surfaced under his rump while pleasing two
    Cherokee ladies in the desert.
Now he's only worried that the Russians may stockpile
    the stuff, and win the world while we're still
    hung up on nuclear illusions.

I have problems with all this since I lived my life
    under the pope,
And while I'm tempted to be St. Paul or Beowulf, or even
    my late bookie, Magpie Jones, I don't need crystals
    once I dig out scapulars and medals,
    and speak in tongues in my garage.
It's not that I lack respect for the entire New Age,
But if Slim and Louie are in on the mystical action,
    You damn well better have one firm, unrelenting hand
    on your wallet.

OF GOD AND PROMISES

Charlie Jordan started a new church,
   And promised the believers a Mercedes,
A villa in Spain, and an Hawaiian vacation.
   Attendance was up sixty-four percent a month
After twelve weeks of preaching personal fulfillment.
   The median income of his flock is $67,000.00.

Sid Gilbert's church leans towards Jaguars
   If appropriate affirmations
Immediately follow acute visualizations.
   After three months Sid had 964 followers
With an increase of four percent a month.
   The median income of his flock is $84,000.00.

My church is into bicycles, canoes, and long walks.
   The median income is not at all impressive.
We do not visualize, affirm, or know what we believe.
   We pray, laugh a lot, and have potlucks once a week.
Membership, besides me, Slats O'Meara, and Johnnycake Jones,
   Consists of two blind lepers and twelve fisherman.

OF ASSORTED GODS

My friends have a variety of gods:

Emery's God has deep set, angry blue eyes, and does not
  take sin lightly. Emery's not much fun at parties.
Gwen's God is hybrid, Methodist above the neck, Baptist
  below the waist. Gwen sings hymns and is a virgin.
Irwin's God is old and likes to be called "Your Honor".
  Irwin curbs his dog and never parks in handicap zones.
Mike's God is a hunk who lifts weights and jogs daily.
  He and Mike run marathons. Hell is being out of shape.
Molly's God is a passionate lover who likes to hug.
  So is Molly, but only Molly gets pregnant.
Al's God is a bright light in the center of his forehead,
  And makes it difficult to drive the freeways at night.
Freddie is an outspoken atheist, but in case he's wrong,
  He sends money to the Little Sisters of the Poor.
Dawn's God is crystal, pyramids, and reads tarot cards.
  She drinks wheatgrass and was a stripper on Atlantis.
My God is Catholic, Jewish, Bhuddist, and likes Emerson.

Lately I've been wondering
  If God ever has an identity crisis.

FORMULA PRAYER

Apparently prayer is a strange and mysterious phenomenon,
  Even trickier than a New York Times' Crossword Puzzle.
Thus, ancient Hebrews, who might well have invented it,
  Butchered bloody bullocks and wailed on stone walls,
Which makes one wonder if God might be an avenging Turk,
  Or had the Kosher wine concession just over the wall.
Christian pleas used every prop from crucifix to candle,
  And made God a Frankenstein of Sunday morning TV,
Or a troubled altar boy who never outgrew his pyromania.

The Holy Rollers prayers are as loud as Quakers' quiet,
  Assuming that God is stone deaf or spaced on valium.
Modern, sophisticated sects who laugh and clap in Church
  Insisting your stomach really is as big as your eyes,
  Or your wallet as big as your imagination, created a
5-step formula stating "He's got it all!", followed by
  "You're Him, so name it, don't doubt, but claim it."
If, however, you ask a million dollars via formula faith,
  You could be paid in Confederate bills, since God's
As literal as computers and has a divine sense of humor.

There are also splinter groups filching from the Greats,
  One telling us to be as stubborn as an unwanted lover
    whose facelift didn't take,
Another insisting it's ours even before we pray for it,
  like a kid who sees through Santa Claus,
  Or those who say only the elect are ever really heard,
    (a not too popular view, though
  It sure built a nice summer place for Johnny Calvin.)

Now my borrowing, non-returnable neighbor, Harry Potter,
  Who wants Joe McCarthy canonized, and Nixon to sue
    Panasonic, and defends Hitler, Stalin, and
  Fast Eddie Malloy, (an obscure tight end who dropped
    3 perfect passes in the '59 City Championship game
    Between Springfield Central and St. Jerome's)
Says it doesn't make a damn bit of difference
  Since the Man from Galilee made it all simple, like
Asking your dad for bread, knowing you won't get a rock.

Which may leave the theology of prayer as opaque as ever,
But reveals a solid fact that might offend 5-stepers:
  I'm sure as hell not God, or neighbor Harry Potter
    Would regularly be munching granite on rye!

12-STEP PROGRAMS

Almost everybody I know is in a 12-step program.
I'm not talking about your run-of-the-mill alcoholics
    and overeaters, your cokers and crackers and
        domestic brand of sexual deviates.
I mean this 12-step thing has covered a lot of ground
    since Christ decided on 12 Apostles and Jacob had
        twelve sons that more or less led
    to the 12 tribes of Israel.
Now there's a whole alphabet of twelvers, some with not
    even twelve members, like the Zebraphobics:
A group of 9 wierdos who in 12 steps paint solid black
    stripes on friendly mules over a period of 12 years.
There's a 12-step group that wants artichokes banned as
    food for anyone but severe obsessives,
Twelve steps for bankers who can't stop saying,
    "Is that right?"
12 steps to help preachers get their throat cleared,

12 more to assist in the destruction of cats or dogs,
  who lick your face at a casual friend's home.
One of the more exciting groups is a solemn faced bunch
  of real sickos learning to ignore bowling on TV.
This has been known, alas, to extend to 13 or 14 steps.

It is predicted that everyone in America will be obliged
    to find a suitable 12-step program
If they are to have any decent socialization at all.
Recently I discovered a 12-step group to limit speed
    readers to twelve books a week,
Groups to allow peeping Toms only 12 blocks of windows,
    and doctors but 12 people in a waiting room.
Oglers may study no more than 12 bodies a day, ski bums
    must buy a 12-only lift pass, and 12-hole golf course
      groups are just around the corner.
Meanwhile, I am devoted to my only 12-step program:
    If I convince 12 total strangers to diet, or lower
      their "big C", for twelve years
I myself can devour all the gravy, chocolate, bread,
    butter, red meat, ice cream, and donuts I want!"

OBITUARIES

Obituaries don't quite cut it
  With their Western Union brevity and censorship
    of levity,
  Listing deeds and degrees and the family we pleased.
    Or tried to.
But who really cares that my buddy, Turk McMahon
  Worked 30 years for General Motors Transport Division,
  Served as president of the Lincoln High booster club,
  Was a charter member of the Elks, Moose, and the
    Toothless Timber Wolves,
Lectured on Nuclear Blasts In Single Family Basements,
And went to the 3rd Reformed Church of the Steel Wigwam?
  (Ignoring the fact that he created one of the reforms
    At Digby's Bar after Monday night choir practice)

Naturally he left kids and assorted grandkids to fight over
  the vintage T-bird on blocks in his garage.
But my real quarrel with the obit is that it doesn't say
  what made him loveable to the gang at Digby's.
Who but his friends know that
  He fed mangy mutts, sick cats, and hungry raccoons,
    till his backyard looked like Animal Armageddon?
  That Turk lovingly meant "Turkey" and he greeted any
    poker hand with: "Isn't that a shit sandwich!"

He paid whores just to give their feet a rest, took
    rebuilt pets to troubled kids or lonely oldsters,
Farted unabashedly whenever he climbed even 3 stairs,
Ate his pie before his roast beef and mashed potatoes,
Sent three blacks and a Mexican girl to college
    on the Turk Plan,
Couldn't resist any cause from Irish Missionaries
    to Save The Aardvark,
And always voted for his wife to be president.
It's bad enough that Riley the undertaker makes every
    corpse look like the son of the abominable snowman,
But Turk's obit sounded like that of any other
    miserable and long suffering executive.

So I'm not immortalized with an inane list of books,
    degrees, clubs, cousins and war records like Turk,
I wrote a practice obituary. It reads:
    He didn't do much but write what he enjoyed, expose
        neo-fascists, understand pain, and mock artifice.
    He loved God and big dogs, tennis and romantic nights
        by the ocean, ice cream, dumplings, lots of men
            and too damn many women.
    He laughed a lot, angered easily, couldn't work for
        anyone, and never held a grudge.
He will be remembered not for books or speeches, but
    Because he cared, saw humor everywhere, refused to
        grow old, never lost hope, and made great chili.
When his books are dust, someone may recall the Halloween
    He played the pope. Two old ladies and an immigrant
        kissed his ring. Only Turk kicked the papal ass.
"May he find a corner in heaven to tell more stories,
    To love and laugh with Fats and Red and Bert, with
        Donna, Lil and Turk—and God, forever!"

One day I heard that a book salesman, with a Mr. Magoo laugh,
had died on skid row in New York. I remembered when he'd read
aloud my first poetry book to anyone who would listen at the
Book Convention in Washington. We became friends, and later
lost touch. I wrote this poem to Al to ease my pain.

OF SALESMEN AND COWBOYS

Well, the cowboys aren't dead by a longshot,
They just wander a wider ravine.
Though their horses are gone
    Save in folklore or song,
The rustlers they meet are as mean.

Their corral is transformed to an airport
Where they ride on the steeds of the sky.
In the snow or the rain
    They will laugh away pain,
And hustle to live till they die.

All their saddles are bulging with samples,
They can market the sun or the shade
And their gun is the mouth
    That can shoot north or south,
If a sale will somehow be made.

There's still a dark bar for the weary
And a fire with shadows to cast,
Where they boast of their wins
    And brag of their sins,
Like the bastard they shot at the pass.

How they laugh to tell of the ladies
That fancied their boots and their rods,
How they loved them all night
    And returned to the fight,
With a whispered "I owe Ya" to God!

While they don't know a cow from a lassoo,
And they'd die in a night on the land,
Yet the same toughened hide
    Speaks of courage and pride,
And the lion-like heart of a man!

The companies they serve are an OK Corral
And Wall Street's an Alamo game.
It's forever High Noon
    In the roadside saloon,
Where they drink to the ghost of Duke Wayne.

Though the bankers shoot faster than Cooper,
And the lawyers make mincemeat of Shane,
The cowboys still ride
    Under sport coat and tie,
And wander their home on the range.

No, the cowboys aren't dead by a longshot.
They just wander a wider ravine.
Though their horses are gone
    Save in folklore or song,
The rustlers they meet are as mean!

SUMMER READING

After fourteen years of marriage and three kids,
  Bonnie decided to do something about her relationship
When Mike took up hang gliding and wind surfing,
  And turned his old VW into a dune buggy.
At the urging of Jane, a liberated and twice
    divorced neighbor,
She began a summer study program in feminist development.
Upon reading *Men Who Hate Women and Women Who Love
Them,*
  She had an affair with a bag-boy at the supermarket.
After a frenzied read of *Women Men Love, Women Men Leave,*
  She burned her cook books and joined a karate class.
She devoured *Smart Women, Foolish Choices,* then sold
  her station wagon and applied to medical school.
She wolfed down *Men Who Can't Love,* sacked the bag-boy,
  And began playing pool two nights a week at a convent.
After an exciting seminar on *Male Dominance From Tarzan
    To James Bond,* she got an apartment,
Gave Mike the kids, and left to be a medical missionary.

A week later, Jane, who recommended the seminars, and
    bought the station wagon,
Moved in with Mike, built a dune buggy, took up hang
    gliding, wind surfing, and auto repair, and
Wrote a bestseller called: *Smart Women Who Never Get
    Left By Men Who Can't Love But Don't Care If
They Pay The Bills, Are Lots of Fun, And Great in Bed.*

IN THE EARLY MORNING HOURS

Sometimes in the early morning hours,
   When I walk the streets and watch the vagrants
     Rise from parks and curbs and deserted buildings,
   When I see them squint leisurely into the sun,
   And hustle up a meal for a few quarters begged
     at the corner,
I wonder if they aren't closer to life than I am.
I have a hard time seeing Christ racing for
     a commuter train,
Or Bhuddha grabbing lunch at the automat.
I can't see St. Francis fevrishly selling commodities,
   Or Ghandi making short term loans at 18 percent.
I wonder if I wasn't born fifty years too soon,
   Or a hundred years too late.
Most of all I wonder if the street people
     Eating what they've got,
     Wearing what they can,
     Going where they want,
Aren't a whole lot closer to life than the rest of us.

OF PORTRAITS
IN PASSING

". . . The freedom that power and possessions
cannot provide,
Is freely given to the little ones in the darkest
corners of the earth,
If only they are trusting child enough to ask!"

THE OLD MAN IN THE PUB

The old man sat alone, reading and reminiscing,
   And visiting with anyone who still
      had anything to say.
Each night a different book, a different passerby
   Who still had time to pause and ponder
      the meaning of a day.
A wrinkled child's eyes,
   Refusing to stare alone in an apartment,
   Reviewing ice-age revelations
      and ancient civilizations
   That reminded how very young he really was.
A fertile mind that made an aging body
   Seem inconsequential.
Still smoking the unfiltered cigarettes
   Forbidden by the doctors that he pallbeared,
And sipping long familiar scotch
   Now softened by a quieting cream he shared
With those not lost in mildewed triumphs and regrets,
   Nor patronized by only indiscriminating pets,
But kissing soft, renewing hands of now familiar ladies,
Still sharing the fresh wisdom
   Of a life well-lived and an old age
Still daring to be filled with people and passion
      given and received,
And the vibrant power of dreams
   Yet unachieved.

ONE LITTLE MAN

One little man making his way in a frightening world,
   Frightening only if he walks all by himself,
Or listens to the hollowness of his own wounded heart.
The only strength is to let go, walking openly with God
   As He gently reveals Himself the way He chooses.
Even now as the Bhuddist priest says his daily prayers
   At some far and indistinguished corner of the earth,
As a meek charwoman of Mecca looks radiantly to the sun,
   And the man of Israel or Ireland seeks his own peace,
A God beyond Sinai and Pentecost, beyond words and icons
   Bends to bless and heal, to make brave and serene.
The freedom that power and possessions cannot provide,
   Is freely given to the little ones in the darkest
     corners of the earth,
If only they are trusting child enough to ask!

I wrote this poem while having a beer with two friends in a Toronto pub. At a nearby table, a young salesman talked excitedly to an older associate who didn't seem to be listening. I saw my father in his face, withdrew from Marge and Jack and wrote this poem.

WILFORD

Wilford's older now and not selling like he used to,
   His face a map of freeways and gravel roads,
   His eyes sad and distant like retirement windows,
   Ears deaf to quadraphonic dreams of a young associate
      spinning schemes transformed to weary reruns,
Skeletal fingers clawing to survive with the remnants
      of tomorrow' s energy.

Passion is gone now, pants baggy with fading memories
      of lusty thighs,
   His walk a tired shuffle pleading for understanding
      and rest, with aching legs dragging him
   Alone from bed to shower without a familiar song.
Stiff hands dress awkwardly in now vintage style, and
   Stir the news dimly *deja vu* into bitter, black coffee.

He is culture's tragedy, selling socks or sleds or
      giraffes, finally
   As extinct and pointless and degraded as he is.
Once he strode boldy, sold vigorously, laughed musically.
   Now bourbon's bite and lonely nights at unresponsive
      bars, with quotas
Roaring in his brain like motel ice machines, have
   Numbed his soul in a cold and paralyzing judgment.

God, how I want to drain his pain and convert his fear
      to laughter,
   Take him to trembling aspen trees turned autumn gold,
Salute brave and barren limbs that clung too desperately,
   And restore the leaves of love and life when only
      winter lies relentlessly ahead.

Soon he will die, twenty years older than his sixty-nine,
   His mind dulled by selling shadows of his own despair,
His heart tensed to protest sham in a sudden explosion,
   And his lurking cancer
Angrily poised to reduce him to his childood name.

Tomorrow he is gone without an epitaph, quotas forgotten,
   Sales unrecorded, love lost and unspoken, and the
Promises he forever made to live another kind of life,
   Will echo silently in a handful of ashes,
Scattered at an unmarked twilight in a nameless wind!

ON THE MORNING OF MY MOTHER'S DEATH

An era has somehow gone—never to return, a last
    touch with parenthood is severed,
Fatherless for years, now motherless finally,
A feeling as profound as a planet spinning
    in space.
Once you were my connection with God, now finally
    returned to Him in whose likeness you were cast,
Every wrinkle forever smoothed, every bruise and
    broken particles of heart forever healed.
Tears transformed to joy, and most of all,
    The surprise, the wondrous surprise that
The God of your childhood never was—only history's
    refuse and anger's shadow, revenge's spectre,
       and misery's creation.
Another God came to greet you this very morning,
    To hold you and love you finally as you deserve.
Now you are close enough to husband and sons,
    Close enough to know that all the pain and time
       was nothing,
Past glories insignificant, the wait worth all of it,
The very globe but a child's top floating in time.
    Fear is turned to love, joined with love!
    All is known, all is safe, all of us forever!

And I can only remember the little girl that
    I could make laugh until she cried.

One hurting Sunday I flipped on TV looking for courage, or at least distraction from pain. A celebrated cleric spoke eloquently of faith, God, and how to get all I could ever want in the world. For some reason I muted the sound, studied the man's eyes, and wrote this poem.

PREACHER MAN

Preacher man smiled painfully atop the Mountain of More,
   And the hungry people waited below to hear of
   Trials and tithing, God and His magical love,
   Moistened with preacher man's own unshed tears.
His eyes said nothing of rhythm or inner rhapsody, of
   The symphony of godly frogs at the edge of a marsh,
   The cry of holy geese on a grey and distant horizon,
   Or sainted cattails shedding silk jackets in the wind,
Without fear or strain, finances or fierce commitment.

Weep for yourself, preacher man! Your well-meant tears
   For the maimed and sick, the poor and dying,
   Are but screams of private pain, the unacknowledged,
   Gnawing illness of a bare and exhausted soul.
Heal yourself, preacher man! Your prayers for health
   And devout rituals for another's healing are but
   The desperate, passionate shouts of a drowning man,
   The final scream of one whose wounds lie unattended.
Save yourself, preacher man! Leave the crowd for a time
   Till you regain a light in your eyes, and the self
   You squandered on the lonely Mountain of More, where
   Greed for God is but a gift-wrapped mask of fear.

Quietly, I left the temple and wandered off to discourse
  With ducks and dogwood trees and laughing crickets
  Who knew at birth what preacher man still must learn:
That the God Who in His image made the grass and apples,
  The subtle smell of a wind caressing cherry blossoms,
  And a delighted squirrel basking in wild aerobics,
Made us as well, and our peace is more like grazing deer
  And wild asparagus, swamp lilies or nibbling gophers,
  Than all the paper flowers blowing from the mountain.

We escape the pent up pain and devouring anxieties,
  Not by texts and tithes and tents of glass and stone,
  But when we can hear the wisdom of the aspen leaves,
And regularly attend summer sermons of the frogs,
  Saved from the Mountain of More and the very sad eyes
  Of an eloquent and deeply wounded preacher man,
  Who showers love on all but his own lost little boy
  Drowning in the eloquence of his own weary words.

> Run from the crowds, preacher man,
>   And let the madness go!
> Talk to the crickets, preacher man,
>   And learn what you already know!

I wrote this poem during a phone call with a buddy trying to choose between 3 different women to take to a beach party in Monterey. He even offered me one of his rejects with a guarantee. I decided it was more than I could handle and went fishing with an old man who still tied his own flies.

ANDY

Andy overwhelms at least three women a week,
    A hobby developed shortly after
        he tired of making model airplanes.
Life is now as dedicated
    to eclectic philanderings,
As any Edison absorbed
    in electric meanderings.
I would be well satisfied with one,
    Only wondering if I must leave the county,
Since my last three dates
    Shook hands at the door
And innocently asked if I knew Andy?

While I was trying to watch Notre Dame play Miami at a Sports Bar, the lady on the next stool gave her views on marriage. She said most men are bastards, and I agreed that by her definition, I surely was. No more would she be made a fool of by some smooth, fly-by-night without a decent portfolio. Since Notre Dame led, I agreed, said I lived off my parents, and wrote this at the half.

BLUEPRINT LADY

Blueprint lady,
   Looking for a future architecturally planned,
   Too afraid to clear the land and take another chance,
      And knowing nothing lasting will arise.
   Pondering the progress every step along the way,
   Weighing and surveying at the end of every day.
      Deprived of midnight madness and surprise.
Blueprint lady,
   Calculating mortgages before the concrete's laid,
   Tabulating painfully the sacrifices made
      When all the other lovers walked away.
   Carefully controlling till all that's left are games,
   So nothing really changes except the list of names,
      Unconsciously forbidding me to stay.
Blueprint lady,
   Desperately begging that your daddy never leave,
   Clinging to the fantasies you really don't believe,
      Just another formulated plan.
   Secretly despising all the bellboys you control,
   Tragically foresaking all the splendor of your soul,
      Afraid to be a woman to a man.

Blueprint lady, all alone again!
Blueprint lady, who the hell needs men?

GEORGE AND JENNY

George and Jenny didn't have much of a marriage,
  But they had one hell of an exciting divorce,
    With passion and orgasmic energy dormant
      Since the early groans of courtship,
    With a rare eloquence of profanity seldom heard
      Even in their most violent of love sounds,
    And a startling recall of each least cruelty
When once even birthdays and anniversaries slipped by
      Like another rainy day in Seattle.
What love, or its fiercest facsimiles had never evoked,
  Now flowed like turbo-powered virginal combustion,
    As a stale and quite commonplace nuptial erupted
Into a really, quite magnificent divorce!

CHESTER

Chester is a philosopher
  Who makes a living selling grubs to fishermen
  And beefsteak tomatoes to housewives
Because the Philosopher's Union dissolved quietly
  Sometime before Sartre and after Socrates.
Yesterday he told me that
  $3.00 stands between a bushy-haired vagrant
    and a bus ticket to Lima, Ohio.
  $30.00 stands between young Lupe Rojas
    and food for two kids.
  $300.00 stands between Ace O'Toole,
    his car payment and a case of beer.
And it's only
  $3,000,000.00 that stands between him
    and the highest paid pitcher in baseball.
  $30,000,000.00 that stands between a bankrupt Texan
    and a decent retirement,
$300,000,000,000 that stands between the American
    government and solvent respectability.
Chester concluded that modern living
  Is just a bunch of zeroes.

OLD MAN

Old man, beaten and fragile and too tired to live,
Your brain scarred and your yesterdays forgotten,
Hoping the doctor will heal what life
    has long destroyed.
Confidence is gone so he becomes a child again.
The nurses and orderlies know as they ease him
    from his wheelchair,
  That he will never be whole again, strapped
    in sameness,
  With pitying or avoiding eyes nodding
    as he rolls by.
He is the symbol of our pain and pressure and
    not enough play.
His mind is lost in distant confusions as he
    mumbles manicly,
  Not even aware that few really care, and if they do,
  Are loathe to express it lest they be lost
In fears of their private madness and approaching death.

TO VASSIE WHO DIED JUST BEFORE CHRISTMAS

Tears of loss mingle with tears of gratitude
　　That there ever was a Vassie to decorate our earth
　　　　Like the forever glow of her final Christmas tree,
And the gentle, guiding light of a child's candle
　　Still shining in apt symbol
　　　　As she slipped privately away.
Even her sudden death was carefully prepared, as if
　　She but adventured on another exciting journey,
Determined to take care of herself till the very end,
　　With pride and courage most lose at the beginning.
Even as she died she dreamed of gift-wrapped love
　　And a warm, fragrant casserole of nurturing life.

Her joyful promenade but danced upon the surface
　　Of the earth, careful not to wear away the soil
　　　　Built by ancient rivers.
Her loving words and easy laughter lent freshness
　　To the air, cautious not to waste the breath
　　　　Born of a thousand flowers.
Like a special seed, guarded for centuries and sown
　　By angels, warmed by the sun itself and washed
　　　　By cleansing summer rains,
She bloomed in forests or in the fragile, shifting
　　Desert sands, in green meadows or in the silted
　　　　Wrinkles of granite mountains.

And blooms still in the laughing eyes
   Of a dancing daughter who learned from her
      The whispered love words of the wind,
The unbridled mirth of stars, the quiet wisdom
   Of the moon, and the joyous embrace
      Of sun and sky, of earth and ocean.

Thus, amid tears of loss that she decided
   To leave us, and the tears of joy
      That she agreed to walk among us,
We are content that she still laughs
   In the memory of friends, still loves
      In the springtime surprise of desert flowers,
And still lives in the joyful eyes
   And generous heart of a unique and beautiful,
      Dancing daughter!

ASSERTIVENESS CLASS

Francine is in her 6th week
  at the *Acme Assertiveness Institute.*
After three weeks she was fired from Harvey's Auto Parts
  after assertively cursing several parts of Harvey.
Two weeks later her father threw her out the front door
  following a viscious attack on her mother's meatloaf.
The next weekend a four-year relationship with Leo ended
  when she broke his ankle during foreplay.
Later, she assaulted a bus driver, threw porkchops at
  her butcher, and punched out Leo's new date
    at an Elks picnic.
In recent weeks, she attacked her hairdresser, slapped
  a Sears repairman, tried to saw her carpenter,
    bit a policeman, and sued her attorney.
Next week she will graduate from *Acme* with honors.
    She is very assertive.

LOVE TREASURE

Little girl, drowned in the wonder of your own eyes,
 Delighted with each heart beat, ecstatically absorbed
  in the mystifying purring of a friendly stray cat,
 Let no one tell you that you are less than wonderful!
 You float above forests and rise with morning mist,
  mock the very sunset in the flush of your living,
 Eclipse a full moon with the joy of your breathing.
 No mountain ever moved me more, no caressing valley
  ever soothed me to greater delight in my own being.
 No love tryst more exciting than a glance at you.
You are a smile that brings laughter to the saddest eyes,
 The peace that moves savage men to discard swords,
  The joy that turns traffic and tenements into home.
 You are the promise that the child I was still is,
  That every dream I've had deserves to be mine,
  Because in shadow and celebration,
   it is already yours!
What parent bold enough to create or even imagine you?
 What teacher rash enough to alter a single syllable?
 What critic arrogant enough to modify an eyelash?
You were all there is already from your very birth!
 The sadness I feel, is that it may take a lifetime
  For a love treasure such as you to know it.

OF GOD AND EAGLE SCOUTS

Michael O'Toole was a devout member of St. Mary's for
   forty-two years,
Made regular novenas, ushered devoutly at the nine
   o'clock Mass,
Guided Eagle Scouts and said the rosary daily in May.
With 8 children in Catholic schools, he took severe
   umbrage at Fr. Day's admission
That the birth control pill may well have been created
   by God Himself in an impulsive gesture of mercy.
He stopped ushering, discarded rosaries, and joined
   a friendly Episcopal Church badly in need of good
   ushers and Eagle Scouts.
Later he became a committed Presbyterian when he read
   in a New Age journal
That a blubbery Henry VIII died of sexual fatigue and
   syphilis,
And left the scouts to explore Avatar and nude therapy.
After a Semi-spiritual affair with a cotherapist,
   He discarded her to pursue the purity of Emerson and
   assorted Transcendentalists.
A revolution broke out when he told Danny Murphy that
   His son's club feet were caused by the wayward
   consciousness of his parents.

He threw it all over when a psychic hairdresser told him
  He had been a revered Bhuddist lama in a former life.
Soon he was channeling, counseling his oversoul, and
  Dropping into exciting past lives by astral travel.
When he cured Lefty Dugan's wife of a carbuncle by
  massaging her left derriere,
He started a Church of his own which artfully interwove
  Luther, Gibran, Marquis de Sade, Hans Solo, and an
    obscure Native American mystic named Horsefeathers.
Attendance fell when an organist ruptured a crown shakra
  with a sacred crystal, and sat naked on the altar
    shouting: "Remember the Alamo!"
So he doffed his tunic, sold his beads, and spent weeks
  in the desert making novenas and saying his rosary.
Last Sunday he ushered joyfully at the nine o'clock Mass,
  And wondered how the Eagle Scouts were doing.

AUTUMN RETURNS

Autumn returns with its sudden explosion of color,
Hardly a suitable announcement of impending death.
Reds and browns and golds incandescent in soft light,
 The evenings gentle and too soon dark.
The air heavier, thoughts grown quiet and serious
 As if the days are devised to ponder
  and the nights to wonder.
I know a man struggling from summer to autumn,
 But painfully, hardly with nature's
  resplendent dignity.
He is more beautiful than he knows, but cannot believe
 That summer is already gone,
Cannot admire the beauty of change and decay no
  matter how colorful.
Strange that nature's annual metamorphosis makes
 Such a feeble impression on our race,
That so few of us flow like oceans or die like flowers.
Even winter covers final harshness with snow
 To hide the fallen branches and decaying leaves, and
Patient evergreens pledge the immortality of trees.
Perhaps that is why so many bypass fall to face winter
 Without a final, dying, pretentious burst of color.

WITH A STYLE

Dennis is a man with his own special style:
  Not dictated by Brooks Brothers or Wall Street
    Or the cliches that frightened men become.
Not going anywhere but where he wants to go,
  Unafraid to walk all alone
As long as the sky still speaks and the night air
  Yet whispers of a dream unfulfilled.
Not fighting life but romancing it
  With laughing eyes and a child's heart,
Every day more startling than he could have planned,
  Straying outside the boundaries of time and space.
Still dreaming beyond the tired, frozen loves
  That finally tolerate routine as happiness,
Accepting age and seeming failure as mere detours
  Along gravel back roads demanding reflection.
Unafraid to dance at dawn and abandon the call of greed,
  To make gentle afternoon love in the meadow.

Most of all, a man with his own style,
  Doomed to hostile tongues and accusing eyes,
Only guilty of living each paragraph of his life.
  And having risked everything every day,
Finally to smile trustingly even at death.

I was asked to honor a doctor friend at his memorial service. He was one of those healers that cared, and my thoughts were too vast to contain. On the morning of the celebration I wrote a poem he'd want to share.

TO JOE, A PHYSICIAN

More than a score of centuries ago, Hippocrates wrested
  medicine from evil spirits and mumbling high priests,
And started a history of healing built on twin pillars
  Of man's own instinctive lust and energy for health,
And the loving care of a most personal practitioner.
  "Our natures are the true physicians of diseases!"
But the war was not easily won, and he toured Greece
  Preaching the simplicity of fresh air, altered diet,
And a change in lifestyles, insisting endlessly:
  "Where love of man abides, healing comes as well."

As centuries passed, his loving simplicity was lost and
  Revived, ignored and taught, mocked and sanctified.
Years of Galen's anatomy and Harvey's circulating blood,
  Of Jenner's vaccinations and Pasteur's microbes, of
Black death and bubonic plagues, small pox and syphillis,
  Years of Roentgen's X-Rays and Curies' radiation,
Of penicillin and Salk vaccine, of Barnhard and DeBakey,
  Cyrosurgery, transplants, anesthetics and pacemakers,
Beyond the wonders of the maddest dreams of Nostradamus.
  But nothing more telling than those Hippocratic words:
"Our nature's are the true physicians of our diseases",
  And "Where love of man abides, healing comes as well."

Now each of us learns anew the healing in our own hands.
  Though doctors betray, there are physicians who heal,
Doctors who sacrifice us to arrogance and avarice, but
  Physicians who hear us and join their loving wisdom
With our own most personal and private path of healing.

And Joe, our friend, who lived and died a physician,
    Humble and real, with all the obvious human failings,
But with a rare gift of love and compassion that felt
    The price of pain and despair, and knew above all
That the most potent pill in any pharmacy is the mind
    And heart of a patient, finding the courage and hope
To renew a tired spirit's waning interest in survival.

This is why we honor him, why we still owe him, not the
    Money he was loathe to ask, nor gratitude we forgot,
But the love that leaps beyond all cultures and faiths,
    And sees in everyone that is sent to us a brother.

Dr. Joe, healer, friend, physician, rest in peace, for:
    When I was starving, you fed me,
    When I was lonely, you held my hand,
    When I wanted to give up, you made me fight,
    When I could only cry, you made me laugh,
    And when my insurance ran out . . .
        You didn't!

DYING OF LONELINESS IN A WORLD FULL OF PEOPLE

Dying of loneliness in a world full of people,
Taking what's offered lest I melt in my own misery.
No real reason for it save honest choices
    made a lifetime ago.
Afraid to hurt a parent's feelings and just as afraid
    to hurt anyone ever since—except myself.
Walking alone amid millions, finally bereft of
    all the illusions,
Wishing only a beer and a ball game could do it again.
Searching everywhere for help, wanting to surrender, to
    give up, but most of all afraid of that.
Wondering not about stars or planets, but how people
    can smile,
Ready to accept any God that helps, still treading paths
    that didn't work before, hoping it'll be different.
Knowing love heals, not knowing how to give or get it,
Surrounded by wonder and beauty, but not able to taste it,
Willing to try anything from medication to snake oil, only
    begging help from power present in my own heart,
And struggling to find the strength to release it.
Knowing finally that there is a Father Who sees and hears me,
    Who cares and guides me on a very rambling road,
Knowing that He is shaping my very life, that His peace
    and joy will not elude me forever,
Even as I am dying of loneliness is a world full of people.

OF ONE UNAFRAID
TO BE HIMSELF

"Failure is only a chance to begin again,
Defeat but a gentle warning to walk another road.
Loneliness an invitation to find a new friend."

FOR ONE UNAFRAID TO BE HIMSELF

There is no failure for one unafraid to be himself,
No defeat for one who does what he can without
  sacrificing the private rhythm of his being,
A rhythm created over centuries and shared with life itself.
Failure is only a chance to begin again,
Defeat but a gentle warning to walk another road,
Loneliness an invitation to find a new friend.
A life built on sand and avarice is the victim
  of every earthquake or avalanche,
Every rise and fall of Dow Jones or a robot's dictation.
Wrap yourself in your own feeble being,
Warm yourself with your own fragile heart,
Defend yourself in peace and silence, and do battle
  with smiles and shrugs
And an awareness of eternal change.
Patience and humility are your impermeable armor,
Love and prayer your impregnable protection.
Your worst adversary is crippled with everyman's fears,
The most severe critic but a raconteur of his own story.
How can there be failure when the ocean still rolls
  towards the land?
And the night still embraces strong and weak alike
  with love?
The morning will come with its soft light
  to offer you a childhood again,
And the wind will sing the gentle rhythm that makes of
  each day a new adventure.

ONCE I GAVE
MY LIFE AWAY

Once I gave my life away
    To parents who dressed their prehistoric wounds
      with my bones,
    To spouses who covered their own ancient scars
      with my flesh,
    To any wayfarer who asked my blood and knew
      what fragile artery to invade.
I gave my life away
    To faceless crowds and impotent powers hiding
      behind history's barricades,
    To bankers and jugglers, well-spoken whoremongers
      and seductive sorcerers,
    To bearded mesmerists and white-robed vampires
      who sucked away my soul.

Now I am ready to reclaim my life,
    To take the final test to determine
      if indeed I am, or fearfully am not,
    With the heavens as trusted allies, and rare friends
      who ask nothing of me but honest courage,
And promise nothing but the freedom to possess my life.

MAN OF CONFIDENCE

How can I tell you that the man of smiles and confidence
  Is frightened now, trembling from the core,
    Uprooted and still pursued by childhood fears
      That refuse to go away?
I want the world to be my friend and all its people,
  Even as the puppy that first licked and loved me
    Like no one else ever has,
    And the friendly echo that lovingly answered,
      Like no one else ever did.
I want you to know that I am not the man I seem,
  Perhaps I never was, and cannot be.
I wake at night afraid, rise up in the morning,
  Filled with some unassailable dread,
    Wondering where I have gone.
Not daring to ask anyone to relieve me of my distress,
  Lest they know that a man does not know what to do,
    Or even how to live.
In the distance, I hear the joy of little children
  Laughing, laughing, laughing, forever laughing,
And I wonder what has happened to me,
  And if ever I was truly a child.

ILLUSIONS

The sun has disappeared, the prism of illusions is gone.
Now I am my own savior,
   Listening quietly to a mysterious voice within,
   Speaking a child's words, and knowing
I will not get a stone when I beg helplessly for bread.
   My cheeks have been dried gulches for years,
      pleading for germinating tears,
   My eyes dessicated swamps longing for
      the gentle spring rains,
   My arms and legs dying trees that struggle
      to recall the green leaves.
   My heart is frozen in some angry Arctic that
      begs repeatedly for summer nights.
I wish there were no pain required to transform a phantom
   man into a laughing boy grown tall,
For the pain of lost illusions is more draining than
   all the accumulated scars of living.
I long to retch the rotteness of undigested memories,
To abort finally some monster child of a rapist's making,
   So that every pore is a womb of new life,
   Every orifice open only to the golden light,
That I might walk freely in love and gentleness, joy and peace,
   Unaccused and unassailable,
      All the days of my life!

LAND OF BLANDNESS

Today I walk in the land of blandness, a land
  without color or form,
Where every house looks alike and every fence
  a prison wall.
The prison is of my own making, since some frozen ducts
  in my brain refuse to flow.
I know the colors will soon emerge from this
  monochromatic madness,
A bird's call or child's voice will be more than a
  stabbing reminder of my own pain.
Fear struggles to envelop me in its claws of despair,
    even as I fight to free myself, and wait another day
      —and then another,
Knowing God is poised to release me once again to walk
    like the child I am of His creation.
Joy lurks behind the grey monotony of depression
      and despair.
This darkness and death was never meant to be and
      thus it will never finally survive.
Victory soon awaits and each passing hour of this pain
    endured is a promise of its approach.

I HAD NOT KNOWN

I had not known there was pain beyond all telling,
   When the mind was ripped from its moorings,
   And every shred of confidence
      Garnered so niggardly through the decades
         As the only antidote to terror
Was scattered and crushed like a tiny wooden boat
   In a raging, moonless sea at midnight.

I had not known there was pain twisting sleep to torment,
   Dreams to the shattered garbage of a lifetime,
   Shredding and magnifying each minute fear until
      There were only monstrous morays to cling to,
      And an insane faith that life must be lived
         No matter this pointless and pervasive torture,
Triggered without apparent warning by timed explosives
   Stored patiently in the secret caches of my brain.

I had not known what depression was when it invaded
   Like the dark clouds and black holes of the universe,
      Swearing in an inverted oath never to leave,
   Nor anxiety, a chaste, clinical word for frozen fear
      Crashing down from the lobes of my reason
         To make peace impossible, freedom unthinkable,
And life itself unbearable, while every cell in my body
   Raged and spasmed in pain no words can describe.

I had not known the horror of hope gone, joy dissolved,
   The simplest task a fearful challenge, when even
      Trees and waterfalls had lost all meaning.
   I was no child stumbling the first time to tie a shoe,
   But a trained, accomplished man draining mightily
      Every drop of courage just to rise from bed
Lest his mangled memories and distorted half-dreams,
   Tear his mind and body to atomic bits.

I had not known there was pain beyond relief,
   Panic beyond redress, horror beyond all comfort,
      Despair beyond the most seductive wooing,
   Reduced to speechless, motionless, helpless terror,
   Left grovelling on the dust of the earth's surface,
All the while blaming and cursing one's self for demons
   Beyond control or culpability.

Now I have known such pain,
   When body and soul were severed, when the sun
      Meant nought but another day of total darkness,
   And only ask of life its most gratutitous and obvious
      pleasures:
   The thrill of dawn, a child's sleep, a song of spring,
   A thousand daffodils, a butterfly, a hawk in the wind,
And to be spared beyond all else that smothering,
   Consuming horror of pain beyond all telling.

DRIFTING DAYS

The days drift slowly by
  As I heal from a soul's wound,
  Unseen and uncontrolled,
And progress is measured not by hours
  But by the growth of trees.
I want to scream for respite,
  Plead for the restoration of what was,
  Curse the skies and seas
And all the powers seen and unseen
  That control my destiny.
Yet, I lie patiently, waiting
  For the darkness to lift,
Scarcely able to beg for relief
  Which I now know will
  Only come when it comes,
Trying not to hate the doctors
  Who blundered and reasurred
  With their faulty medication,
Struggling to believe each new man
  Who seems to know my suffering
  And its final cure.

I had never known one could suffer like this,
   Never really appreciated
   The breadth of my joy.
Now I cling tenuously to the hope
   That once again I will laugh
   Like I did since childhood,
When at the very moment of true healing,
   The pain will be forgotten forever.

I KNOW

I know I should have been a doctor, a dentist,
A beloved Mr. Chips with tenure exuding from his ears.
Even a mechanic or an architect, a clever lawyer,
   a builder of tracts or an intractible banker.
Safe jobs, predictable, that keep a man in one place
   and increase his net worth year after year.
Certainly not a poet flitting from town to town,
Struggling to make sense of beauty and
      unspeakable tragedy.
I could have been one hell of a gardner,
   though I never liked petunias much.
Now it seems too late and I can only hope
   that soft music rings in my ears till I die,
And that iambic computers don't replace poets.
But if so, I'll just have to take another look
   at petunias.

OF SOVEREIGNTY

Preserving sovereignty and joy in a world
   of hungry tongues,
Nibbling at first, and then devouring all who stand
   firmly on two legs.
The foundation people, rooted in concrete,
Abandoning illusions for the messages of their own hearts,
Walk proudly and bravely amid those who have made of fear
   an invincible tyrant.
Life is not an enemy, not a ghoul of hidden terror,
Not a trembling sychophant who cannot endure the truth.
Life is a friend, a flowing river, a caressing wind
   who only asks that we
Do not blindly fight the timeless currents of
    an eternal order.
What man can assault the hurricane? Embrace the tornado?
Stand unmoved before the angry gale that tears ships
   apart like puny balsalm?
Who can finally endure the teeth of the ocean's waves,
   the roar of a swollen river's rage,
Floodwaters bursting bonds to devour all in their path?

The brave man only weathers the storms he must,
   but does not make of life itself a storm.
He sails with the torrential winds, floats gently with
   the fiercest waters,
Knowing that even the typhoon battering his soul,
   will finally grow silent,
Because He Who tamed the winds of the Lake of Galilee
Still walks by whatever name in the deepest caves
      of his soul.
The brave man walks with quiet certainty in any sudden
   cyclone, preserving his sovereignty and joy
In a world of fearful, devouring tongues!

I CANNOT SETTLE
FOR SAWDUST

I cannot settle for sawdust
As long as the feeblest elm tree
   Rises bravely amid the chilling granite rocks.
Silently we stand together, arms and leaves entwined,
   Ready to share the cold, torrential rains,
   Ready to confront the north wind's rage,
     To build a home where truth lives
     And freedom is a right from birth.
I have softly traced your leaves a hundred times
   Know every scar on your bark,
   Know exactly how you feel in darkness and sunshine.
I want to find love together,
   Search the world hand in hand like children.
I am but a boy looking for a girl,
   Still a lonely child in an empty neighborhood,
   Waiting for a chosen friend to move in next door.
And the God I reluctantly gave away in ritual and law,
   Returns in simple garb and gentle shadow,
     To whisper the way.
But I cannot, will not settle for sawdust,
As long as the feeblest elm tree
   Rises bravely amid the chilling granite rocks.

IT IS NOT FAIR

It is not fair to live but one life, knowing what I do.
I would draw a curtain on the past and emerge unscarred,
   Finally aware of when to love and when to move on.
I would have a thousand conversations and never lie,
   Never again regret yesterday or fear tomorrow.
Death would not frighten me for I would be totally alive
   At every moment, accepting each decade as it is dealt,
Not running from pain to suave and myopic magicians,
Nor ignoring fear till it finally ossifies to strangle me.

Some seem to live so well
   To pass each barrier with wisdom and affection.
I have not been so fortunate:
   A mountain built to conceal an earthquake
   A dam erected to restrain the flood waters
   A hurricane racing madly when I wanted to walk
   A hissing tornado when I ached for silence.
Now I have decided to live another life,
   Beginning this day, this very moment,
An adventurer beyond calculation, a maverick
   Bereft of any destination but joy.

All the wisdom I have gathered from pain and misfortune,
   All the wounds endured and inflicted,
   All the dark and endless nights of fear and sadness,
   All the risks never taken and the loves never known
Are but the birth pangs, brief and soon forgotten
   Of a new and never ending life.

WORDS, WORDS, WORDS!

Too many words assaulting my mind,
Pointless, pointed, and pleading words,
   Words beyond all counting or caring,
   Words beyond sounding or sharing,
Words piled upon words until I cannot hear my soul.
   Words drowning spirits and crowning empty lives,
   Patter of words, rattle of words,
      Words, words, words doomed forever to be unheard.
      Words, words, words pouring out like chaff
         in a harvest of nothingness.
Spare me from chattering, battering, shattering words,
Endless, friendless, empty words, words, words,
   Until I never want to speak again or listen.
What is the point? When words have currency and truth
         and joy
   Are lost in a forest of echoing words, words, words?
   Even the birds chatter instead of singing.
And I run to rest in the sounds of whispering palms,
   And the gentle cadence of the ocean,
      In the silence of the sky
And the endless galaxies beyond words, words, words!

THE SAME FEAR

The same fear pursuing me since childhood, demanding
  I give up my dreams or die,
Swearing I cannot make it alone, and living out the fear
  of parents every day.
I have walked to the innermost chamber where the core
  of it lies forever in wait,
Hissing with fire and snarling that there is no freedom
  and joy for a terrified little boy.
So long this fear has ruled my life!
  So long it has led me where I didn't want to go!
  So long it has turned the joy of sunrise into the
    terror of self torment.
All the exits marked along the way proved no escape,
All the voices shouting: "Here is happiness!" proved
  to be false and unavailing.
Still I hang on after the detours and dreams of peace.
Just when I think I have it in my hand, just when the
  shadows and evil spirits are finally gone,
They return in new guise and with greater energy!

They are *not* stronger than my hand in Yours!
There *is* the tomorrow that I forever dream of!
There *is* the love that my finest hopes have promised!
Otherwise, why have You guided me when long ago I
  could have fallen into the final abyss?
You lifted me when I could not take another step,
  gave me a hand when all was barren and void.

My God, dearest God! I will not be abandoned by You,
   no matter the poverty of my words or the feebleness
      of my prayer.
You are not like the rest! You do not extend your hand
   only to drag me where I do not want to go,
But to lead me where peace and celebration are!
   So many voices tell me what I must do!
   So many prophets screaming: "Here is the Christ!"
   So many directions leading in circular surrender!
I put myself in Your hands beyond sects and theologies,
   beyond systems and cleverness and dire proclamations,
For You alone can draw order from this mounting chaos.
I will walk a path of silver light amid the shadows.
   Fill me with love and hope and courage!
   Fill me with wisdom and strength and confidence!
Hold me in Your arms, just for today, and take me
One step closer to the end of the tunnel of fear
   into the fullness of Your consuming love!

WHEN THE DARKNESS COMES

When the darkness comes, I now know that it will pass,
And when I feel alone and unloved, I can sing a new
   Litany of all those who truly love me.
God and I are on better terms of late, and though He
   Speaks more softly than distant violins,
His words are clear and unmistakeable
   When I am still and serene enough to hear.
He has sent me love when I least expected it,
Granted warmth when the rain was relentless
   And unforgiving,
And offered me serenity amid confusion and desperation.
I walk more humbly now, but gradually more hopefully.
There is a corner of my heart that ever clings to life
   And a dim dream that will not disappear
      No matter the past mistakes or future fears.
I, like you, have done the best I knew how.
   What seemed like anger was only hidden hurt,
And what wounds I caused were only the flailing
   Of a frightened warrior struggling to hang on
      to his own life.
All this I can forgive, and hopefully be forgiven,
But most of all, when the darkness comes,
   I now know that it will pass.

TODAY

Today I stand like God astride the sky and chaos,
   Creating my own world in seven days or seven centuries,
   Bringing the sun into focus, and celebrating
   The golden aspen trees and blushing peonies
     That fall from my fingertips,
   Gathering swans and fawns from the dust,
   Building orange mountains at twilight,
     And carving out peaceful valleys.
   Boldly I bid the splashing, silver rivers
     To fill the ocean
     And set in motion the repititious waves.
   Each tulip and crocus is my own creation,
   Each wooded path and creeping vine is my invention.
At the end of the final day, I lovingly create myself,
   And fashion from the rib
   That guards my heart, a bride.
Only then, like God, I rest!

FINALLY...MY OWN GENTLE PLACE

"I no longer want the whole world, just my own
  Gentle place of service and love
And the courage and strength from God to do
  Today and tomorrow,
Whatever I was meant to do."

FINALLY

Finally I want so little of life,
Merely to let me run free,
To greet each day with some excitement and new found hope.
I ask not fame or fortune, but some quiet tranquility
   that lives within me at all times,
And does not fear loss or storm, life or death, or
   whatever is mine to confront.
I cannot recall the past or remake it, I cannot live
   with regrets of what I have or have not done.
I can only hold on to a Father's hand knowing His
   strength is mine.
Life is this moment, the lady walking the dog, cars
   parked by the side of the road,
Lovers holding hands briefly in the morning chill.

Fear is a strange and persistent enemy—I find it hard
   to fight him directly lest he overwhelm me.
I let him pass through my being and know that he has
   no more currency
Than strange sounds I heard in the basement as a child.
I've learned too much for fear to hide it under a bushel.
I've travelled too many roads finally to turn back,
   loved too much to be denied.
I no longer want the whole world, just my own gentle
   place of service and love,
And the courage and strength from God to do today
   and tomorrow whatever I was forever meant to do.

CLOUDS

Letting life happen as it will,
Like a directionless cloud that moves in majesty,
  And thus finally with wisdom.
Passing through other clouds and even mountains
  Without anger.
Drawing water without greed, and showering the earth
  Without pride or hostility.
Simply a cloud floating wherever it must float.
Grown graceful in every wind, and darkened
  Without losing grace,
Rising and falling as is destined,
Content with the sky's gift of space
  With no thought of replacing the sun,
And gratefully enlightened by the moon.
  Friend of the earth and everyone,
A dancing, smiling, silent, balloon
  Without protest or pretence,
  Without ambition or lost innocence,
Letting life happen as it will.

I HAVE SLEPT

I have slept countless nights with monsters
    at the bottom of the sea,
Explored the eerie darkness of the ocean floor
    for days on end, plumbed
The core of black holes to challenge serpents,
And invaded all the sinuous caverns of my own mind
    until fear became a friend and loneliness
      a trusted and wise companion.
I have died and returned to life. Thus, there is
    nothing left to see, nothing left to terrify
    save attachment to power and possessions,
Or addiction to a friend who doesn't understand.
No honor can replace freedom, no emolument
    can replace love.
Even God cannot replace me!
Now it does not matter if I am known or unknown,
    victor or vanquished.
All I have learned is to admire the sunrise
    and surrender myself to the sunset,
To realize that giraffes and grasshoppers
    knew all of this before I did,
Without pain or effort.

THE GOD WITHIN

The God within teases like a seductive lover,
   With intermittent orgasms of light amid darkness,
And sporadic love bites amid capricious abandonments.
Just when I decide to walk away in pain and loneliness,
   He whispers bewitching words of affection and hope
      to calm ancient fears and restore dying dreams.
I am filled with a clear vision of what my life can be,
And see myself tented with Him in a green, peaceful valley
      of caressing clouds, and a bold, embracing sun.
So I remain for another day, another warming touch,
   Knowing that a life is being totally reconstructed
   By an honest architect of creative and unending love.
The nuptials are spoken only when they are spoken,
   Unmoved by the frantic timetable of my own anxieties,
   As I stand by and wonder at the teasing seduction
      of the playful, loving, joyful God within.

I DON'T PRAY SO VERY WELL

I don't pray so very well
  With all the levels of divine contact newly devised
And all the assorted certainties of those who know
  Far more about God than perhaps He does Himself.
I'm still in the back pew with the publican,
Struggling to believe, pushing through today's pain,
  And worried about what's in store for tomorrow.
I hang on to simple things like a Father Who never
  Gives a stone when I ask Him for bread.

Some of the greatest gifts I received were when
  I never asked at all,
When a loving, unseen hand took me safely along
  Some precipices I'd not like to walk again.
God is still a mystery to me and my faith is probably
  As weak as any man's alive.
But I never quit believing in love and joy and serenity,
And knowing that somehow I am a favored son
  Whether I deserve it or not.
Our relationship keeps getting simpler:
  I picture the kind of man I really want to be,
And in bits and pieces He gives me the help to be it.

WANDERING THE BACK ROADS

Wandering the back roads
  Where peace greets me at dawn,
  And love and joy are waiting
    In gentleness at twilight
In the stillness of friendly hills and tranquil valleys.

Abandoning the highways
  Where the din of traffic stifles dreams
  And hurry and sadness abandon me
    To sameness and despair
Along the frenzied boulevards speeding nowhere.

Wandering the back roads
  Where I am reborn in serenity and laughter,
  Where a frightened child grown listless,
    Now rebounds in renewed energy and
The passionate ecstasy of a free and creative life.

Abandoning the highways
  Where the nameless, lonely ones
  Are lost in a faceless, winter fog
That leads finally to the desolate cities
Of empty excitment and premature death.

Now life is my friend
  Whispering secrets never shared before,
  Transforming time into the ease of forever,
Where I see beauty privately fashioned,
  Hear music spontaneously composed
And smile helplessly—wandering the back roads.

LET THEM COME

Let the words come like the wind from within
    Without struggle or cleverness,
    Without efforting or fearfulness.
Let them come!

Let the truth come like the waves from within
    Without wrinkled brow or strain,
    Without worry or concern.
Let it come!

Let the answers come like the clouds from within
    Without hurry or distress
    Without the loss of cheerfulness.
Let them come!

Let life come like the earth from within
    Without impatience or demands,
    Without anger or commands.
Let it come!

Let God come like the sun from within
    Without fear or control,
    Without tension or wrinkled soul.
Let God come!

THE DAY COMES

The day comes without schedules or warning
   To tell of life again and morning unexpected.
It is always a surprise, life I mean,
Never what I anticipate, and seldom what I ask.
I have wanted a thousand things
   Enough money to sail the seas forever
   Enough friends never to know loneliness
   Enough sex languorously given in sunlight
   Enough praise never to feel emptiness and sadness.
Now I only ask
   That a tree smile at me
   The sky never hide its face again
   The song of a bird heard in reverence
   And a gentle lover who knows
      each mounting fear, each budding joy.
No longer can I attack life. It is the master,
   No matter what the young, unscarred heroes say.
I am but leaves and wind, clouds and rain,
   Sun and sand and iris at the edge of the garden.
I am lilac trees and cherry blossoms,
   Lilies of the valley and paths of violets in forests.
No more, no less.
   My heart sings when it sings,
   Weeps when it weeps,
   And loves when it can.
As the day comes—without schedules or warning.

GREY WHALES

The grey whales screaming plaintively into the night,
  Weeping, laughing, moaning, loving,
Begging a mate to hear their pain and longing,
Begging a whole world to understand
  Their journey from Arctic shores, their flight
    from human enemies,
Recalling their ancient courage and drawn to
    secret lagoons,
Memories borrowed from long before the birth of man,
And hoping that a tender heart will finally hear
  And shatter the loneliness of their long excursion.
As predictable as waves and the tides that guide them.

Somehow I share their profound memory, as if an angel
  directs me from the primal light of creation,
As I now make my way through each year of my life,
  Weeping, laughing, moaning, loving,
And hope that I will finally be led to a safe harbor of
  intimacy and joy,
That my pulsing, silent screams will be heard,
And I will make the endless journey
  In a deep abiding love,
In eternal union with the whales.

THE HEALING

The healing of the deepest wounds seems slow,
But time is of little consequence for all the joys
   that lie ahead.
So much time spent walking through life, going where
   you never were.
Now, at last you are alive in each moment,
Taught by pain and the lonely separation from yourself.
Once you wanted it all, now you know that all
   lives in each honest moment.
Excitement and exuberant echoes are no match
   for serenity and gentle peace,
A contented heart, a trusted friend, and finally time
   to look long enough to see.
It is a loving God Who hands you a custom cup to drink,
A brave and loving man who drinks it all and lives.
   Take back the eyes that were blinded by hurry
     and preoccupation!
   Take back the ears that were deafened by
     dischordant sounds!
   Take back the words that only echoed in the wind!
Now you are your own, and patient healing will teach you
   What no master ever did or could.

Information About Books, Tapes And Appearances By James Kavanaugh

In September 1990, all rights to James Kavanaugh books were purchased by Steven J Nash who is now the exclusive publisher of Kavanugh's books and tapes. For information, write:

STEVEN J. NASH PUBLISHING
P. O. Box 2115   Highland Park, IL 60035
or call: 1-708-433-6731

BOOKS BY JAMES KAVANAUGH

There Are Men Too Gentle To Live Among Wolves. The James Kavanaugh classic in its 67th printing! He writes: "I am one of the searchers... We searchers are ambitious only for life itself, for everything it can provide... we want to love and be loved, to live in a relationship that will not...prevent our search, nor lock us in prison walls..."

Will You Be My Friend? *(57th printing)* Kavanaugh writes: "Friendship is freedom, is flowing, is rare... It trusts, understands, grows, explores, it smiles and weeps. It does not exhaust or cling, expect or demand. It is— and that is enough—and it dreams a lot!"

Laughing Down Lonely Canyons. Kavanaugh confronts human loneliness and fear. He writes: "This is a book for the barely brave like me who refuse to abandon their dream... It is for those who want to make of life the joy it was meant to be, who refuse to give up no matter the pain..."

From Loneliness To Love. Kavanaugh writes: "To move from loneliness to love means to take a risk, to create the kind of personal environment and support we need. This is a book of hope and reassurance that love is available and loneliness can end."

Search: A Guide For Those Who Dare Ask Of Life Everything Good And Beautiful. *(Prose)* "**Search** provides 12 proven principles to move from self doubt through self awareness to self love. It is a celebration of one's creativity and unique beauty, rising from practical psychology to the spiritual power of our Inner Being in a journey to wholeness."

Today I Wondered About Love. *(formerly, Faces In The City)*. This book was written in San Francisco and captured the soul of that most human of cities. Herein are some of Kavanaugh's most profound and gently humorous reflections on the man-woman experience and the quest for personal freedom.

Maybe If I Loved You More. These passionate, lyrical poems confront forces that numb our senses and corrupt our values. Kavanaugh challenges us to be fully human, to move past private fears to simplicity and joy: "So much of life is spent trying to prove something...Maybe if I loved you more, I wouldn't have to prove anything!"

Sunshine Days And Foggy Nights. This work contains Kavanaugh's most tender love poems, like the wondrous *Fragile Woman*: "too tender for sex, who will surely die—if tonight I do not love you." He speaks of the energy of any creative life: "The work I find most significant drains the least energy...my distractions are usually more creative than my resolutions."

Winter Has Lasted Too Long. Kavanaugh sings of personal freedom and real love in a superb preface: "We shall be as free as we want, as mad as we are, as honest as we can. We shall accept no price for our integrity...This book is a heart's recognition that truth matters, love is attainable, and spring will begin tomorrow."

Walk Easy On The Earth. A book inspired by Kavanaugh's years spent in a remote cabin in the California gold country. "I do not focus on the world's despair, I am forever renewed by spring splashing over granite rocks, or a cautious deer emerging into twilight. I know then that I will survive all my personal fears and realize my finest dreams."

A Village Called Harmony-A Fable. A powerful, eloquent prose tale that touches the deepest chords in the human struggle of lust and love, passion and peace. Dear Abby says: "It is a powerful tale of our times. A classic! I loved it!"

Celebrate The Sun: A Love Story. A moving prose allegory about the life of Harry Langendorf Pelican, dedicated to "those who take time to celebrate the sun—and are grateful!" A stirring tale that touches the very core of love—loving oneself.

The Crooked Angel. James Kavanaugh's only children's story tells of two angels "with crooked little wings" who escape from isolation and sadness through friendship and laughter... A particular Christmas delight. Says Goldie Hawn: "My children loved it! So did I."

Tears And Laughter Of A Man's Soul. James Kavanaugh writes: "Men are not easy to know, even by other men...It's a rare woman who understands men...we hope another marriage, a secret affair, or more income will revive us...ingrained habits only assume a new addictive form, depression fills a vacuum of dead dreams...the path to freedom and joy is more exciting than difficult."

Quiet Water: The Inspirational Poems Of James Kavanaugh. In this powerful new edition of his own favorites, Kavanaugh gives hope and courage when life's most difficult passages seem impossible to endure. He writes with the wisdom and compassion born of his own painful discovery of the path to peace and joy. A perfect gift for a struggling friend!..."There is quiet water in the center of your soul..."

Mystic Fire: The Love Poems Of James Kavanaugh. All the passion, romance, and tenderness, as well as the humor and pain of love unfold in this beautiful new edition of Kavanaugh's favorite love poems. Men and women of any age, will find herein the perfect gift, on any occasion, celebrating the expression of love... "Love grew like some mystic fire around my heart..."

In addition to his books Kavanaugh also has a selection of poetry readings and lectures on audio/video tape available through Steven J. Nash Publishing.

About the author

James Kavanaugh exploded onto the American scene in 1967 with **A Modern Priest Looks At His Outdated Church.** The New York Times called it "a personal cry of anguish that goes to the heart of the troubles plaguing the Catholic Church. "Though a gifted scholar, with degrees in psychology and religious philosophy, he surrendered his priestly collar and doctoral robes to become a "gentle revolutionary".

Twenty years ago in a decrepit New York residence hotel, Kavanaugh rejected lucrative offers to write what publishers wanted. "Feasting", he laughs, "on bagels, peanut butter, and cheese whiz", he wrote his first poetry book, **There Are Men Too Gentle To Live Among Wolves.** The book was turned down by a dozen publishers, only to sell over a million copies.

Wayne Dyer captures his power:

"James Kavanaugh is America's poet laureate. His words and ideas touch my soul. I can think of no living person who can put into words what we have all felt so deeply in our inner selves."

A dozen poetry books followed, as well as powerful novels, prose allegory, and his best-selling **Search**, a guide for personal joy and freedom. The rebel priest became the people's poet, singing songs of human struggle, of hope and laughter, of healing that comes from within.

James Kavanaugh possesses a charisma that excites audiences with passion and humor. He loves wandering, tennis and trout fishing, the cities and wilderness, people and solitude.